A Fire in the Hill

Poems

Steven Huff

Blue Horse Press Redondo Beach, California 2017

A Fire in the Hill

Steven Huff

Blue Horse Press
318 Avenue I # 760
Redondo Beach,
California   90277

Copyright © 2017 by Steven Huff
All rights reserved
Printed in the United States of America

Cover art: *Santa Rosa Barn at Twilight*
Blue Horse Press archives (2016)

Editors: Jeffrey and Tobi Alfier
Blue Horse Press logo: Amy Lynn Hayes

ISBN 978-0692962848

for Betsy

and in memory of Kurt Brown

Other Books by Steven Huff

Poetry:
The Water We Came From
More Daring Escapes

Short Fiction:
A Pig in Paris
Blissful and Other Stories

Nonfiction:
Knowing Knott: Essays on an American Poet (editor)

Contents

Hungry

A Fire in the Hill / 1

For the Cleaners / 2

fMRI / 3

Ouzo for Breakfast / 4

Time was / 5

In the Hall of Rashes / 6

Continental Drift / 7

Merton, Lax and My Father / 8

Hungry / 10

An American Uncle / 11

Great Pyramid / 13

Demolition / 14

Insurance / 15

Estate Sale / 16

On Thumbs: After Montaigne / 17

Mortifications

The Holy Re-runs / 21

The Cold / 22

You'll Get Your Turn / 23

Famous singers die / 24

There's no heaven anymore, I'm told / 25

All There Is / 26

Adam / 27

After Samson, blinded, pulls down the temple / 28

The Accidental Saint / 29

Earth and Names / 31

Late / 32

Mortification / 33

Or Not

Our school burned down every June / 37

Brought in for Questioning / 39

Homage to The Night of the Iguana / 40

Or Not / 41

Horses / 43

What Did You Love about Your Town? / 44

A Lucky Man / 45

Safe / 47

The Editor's Assistant / 49

All Formulae Absent / 50

Metastasis / 51

Regarding the Old Faker / 53

Autumn Inventory / 55

A Long Day / 57

Poor / 58

Rolling Away / 59

Feral / 60

Sometimes I forget the universe and wander the ocean floor / 61

A Flying Fish / 62

About the Author

Acknowledgments

Hungry

A Fire in the Hill

Cain the first killer also built the first city, which probably began
from a fire in a hill where they melted metals from the wild rocks
poured into molds, which meant that they made the first *this*, the first *that*.
In my old town whatever we found in the fridge we crammed
into the blender with a little whiskey, the age of real invention
seemed over. So, we waited for the alarms of passage: you learn
to drive and someone gets pregnant and someone rolls a tractor over
on himself. But I'd have died for that fire in the hill, that bubble of luck
when you're stone ignorant and anything is possible. Decades later
I walk childless back to the old house, look in the window at
the collapsing wallpaper, the wires hanging from the ceiling in the room
where I strangled from the croup until I turned luminous blue
and thought I saw Jesus. Maybe I didn't, it might have been a mental
construction like one has near death, part from His living room portrait
plus a parade of stories, a little gold in my dream-pan. So I
wait another lifetime for the *numinous*, but whenever I write that word
a syllable falls off, or it lacks certain authenticating serifs.
We crammed everyone into a car with too much whiskey, but we were
lucky. Or maybe we weren't. Maybe luck was a mental construction
of barely missed bridge abutments and the stone ignorance of what
was possible. Maybe the age of luck was over and we were just
a speeding pinball of boys who didn't see Jesus, didn't get arrested,
eventually poured into molds, the same old *this*, same old *that*.

For the Cleaners

One day we'll be forced to send a team to space to clean up the garbage,

to recycle dead communications satellites crowding

the outer perimeter of our gravity,

or hang a weight from their frames and let them plunge into the Pacific,

blow up an errant spy satellite that stopped watching North Korea

but ogled France or Hawaii, dead ships that could wipe out

your city if allowed to tumble to earth.

We'll have personal satellites by then, I'll be able to watch you sleep

until I get bored, then beam into your dream and turn it erotic,

or comic erotic, or right in the middle of your dream I'll kick

you out of it and make you buy it back.

We'll have more damned fun with those satellites

until we're forced to send the cleaners to space.

fMRI

Our fMRI images find that love is a glimmer in the same

lobe of the brain from which spring spiritual experiences,

even the mystical ones. They're only a light born in the belly

of one of your brain's billion fireflies, though when you love, one

glimmer

enlists the sympathy of another: love lights the firefly

of Eros from amid the vowels of the right cortex,

while across the Jordanal Longitudinal Fissure

warning and worry are building their own little blazes: *Wear a condom.*

Now look, *look* at these images, the blinking spectrum of colors:

here come the brain's fireflies of orgasm, epiphany and transcendence.

But keep in mind, they're only predictable glimmerizations.

You're not in love, God never spoke to you, and science is busy

From out of the cranial smoke come the fireflies of emptiness.

Ouzo for Breakfast

Only fools and charlatans know and understand everything, said Chekov.
Ishmael said, Only I am escaped to tell thee.
But there may be no *only* anymore. Where have you seen a real one lately?
The world is stuck on iterations, chorus and echo,
skeins of microsecond duplication, the yada yada laser.
One hardly believes one who says, Only whackos drink ouzo for breakfast,
or, Only an ignoramus disobeys the gastroenterologist.

Give me a rebirth of wonder *only* in the nominative-singular-present,
a world where reliable *onlys* still come to the door
like an encyclopedia salesman bearing astonishment. I want to say,
Only I can love you the way I do, and, Only you are real to me.
I want to say, Only I am escaped to tell.

Time was

when a sad man, or an anxious one, they put such a fellow

to work on a ship and he vanished from land.

The moon at sea arrived every night to check on his soul

and there was Tangier for his shadow.

In the desert too God could really have at you,

but nowadays one eats lunch in Thailand and defecates it in London

or New York, and the satellites push the stars aside the better

to track you. I once cried all the way from Miami to Istanbul.

Is mobility a sleep-walk now? I had my hand up

to ask that question, but the world shrugged and moved on

before I got an answer. And another one: *Doctor*, I said,

is it true the breath is the tide of soul between body and mind

as the Greeks believed (some of them anyway)?

I found out it's a question long proven empty.

Too late to send the interrogator to sea.

I still want a Tangier for my shadow, but with Bowles gone

the world has moved on. I'll ask a satellite to find me another.

In the Hall of Rashes

I went there to use the men's room since none was closer.
I passed displays of diaper rash & shingles, second-stage syphilis,
hives & measles. The older I get the more I have to pee
& I wander into places like this. Poor Job was pictured with
weeping carbuncles—do you think I liked looking at that? & those
other guys in the men's room wanted to show me their rashes,
& me to show mine. & they wanted my phone number.

Continental Drift

California and Japan move closer every year by a few inches.
But eventually we'll fall into each other's arms. Remember,
mutability rules the universe, and the process of crossing
the water might speed up, be finally like standing
in a ferry bow as it docks with a final bump, the gate
flung open and the crowds commingling. Like newlyweds
we'll combine our linen, keep the good furniture
and send the bachelor-threadbare stuff to the curb.

Sex will happen fast, but combining currencies, responsibilities,
slaughterhouses and debts will take longer. But scientists
say we'll eventually pull apart again. We'll see a big crack
in the ground and ignore it for a while. But soon we'll wave:
God be with you. At last, on our own, the vast water,
the moon admiring itself in the night sea, siren fish singing.
The sun saying, I told you so, California.

Merton, Lax and My Father

Thomas Merton and Robert Lax used to drive over to Bradford PA
From Olean for a night out in the bars, looking for girls, hitting
The movie theaters. It was 1938, Bradford was a money-jingling
Oil town then. Merton was working on his masters thesis on Blake,
Not yet a monk, had just found that Blake had read
The Bhagavad-Gita and the Far Eastern mystics.
Lax, not yet self-exiled, not yet the poet but following a holy inner
Lure, and any girl who matched his stare. I was born in Bradford,
But not for another eleven years. My father was driving
A truck for Bradford Laundry and taking a correspondence
Course in refrigeration. He was that rare guy who actually finished
And aced such chances he found advertised in the back pages
Of *Argosy* and *The Bradford Era*. Not yet in the Army,
Had not gone to the Pacific. Had just played his first game of pool
And wondered why the preacher was so down on it. He didn't drink,
So he wouldn't have run into the pair in a bar, arm wrestled
With the one-day famous monk. But he went to the movies. Bunches
Of adventure films hit the screen that year: *Adventure in Sahara*,
Adventures of Marco Polo. *Blondes at Work* with Glenda Farrell,

Bluebeard's Eighth Wife with Claudette Colbert. He didn't dance
Like Merton and Lax, but he probably saw *Swing Your Partner*
With Humphrey Bogart. I know this is a stretch, but I imagine
Him in row seven with his arm around my mother, watching some silly
Flick like *Boys Town* with Spencer Tracy, and turning around
To the two clowns laughing and throwing popcorn and saying,
Knock it off, you guys. He had a stare that could make you break out
In boils, but he would have been a mere silhouette to them.
Hey you bozos, I said knock it off.

Hungry

I was skinny enough once that I broke into my mom and dad's trailer
by squeezing between the louver windows like a squirrel
and popping the screen. My wife had left me and I kept
forgetting to eat. But soon I had a new woman and my belly
grew again like a moon that I held in my lap as I drove to her house,
the eyes of hungry deer coming out of the woods into my headlights
like they wanted to die. Once, out on that crooked road
my car coughed like a deer and rolled to a stop.
Love was expensive and I'd tried to get by another night
without buying gas. Hungry now, again, I wondered if she'd
come looking for me, or let me die like my battery, its juice
draining out of my radio with the ball scores, the weather report,
a barking preacher, and America's best burger just ten miles up the road.

An American Uncle

Most Americans I know had an uncle like yours
who drove a red car with a leaky gas tank that burned up
one afternoon when some woman leaned on it
and lit her cigarette. He played poker and screwed, this uncle.
You had other uncles who screwed and nothing much
happened, but locusts rose from the abyss when this uncle did,
and the bells in town went clunk. You found him
lying on the couch one morning, his face a raincloud-blue,
and you asked your mom as you dressed for school,
Is he dead? And she said, Why, no, *no*, though you could tell
she wasn't so sure. This uncle wrestled the devil away
from the door of your house—he was the only one around
who could do such a thing, and when they tumbled over
the grass they threw off jagged splinters of light. He was
named for a Civil War general, but he didn't care. When he
wasn't lying deathly on the couch he was pouring cement
for a dam in Ecuador or Idaho. He coaxed you into
reading *Ulysses* and he called you up from Bora-Bora to ask
if you'd finished it yet, and he knew you were lying.
Shot down in WWII, he parachuted into a French whorehouse.
He taught you to love Roosevelt, and Billy Holliday.
Unhappy women took turns marrying him and each of them

knew all the others. Your uncle, who never lived anywhere in particular as far as you knew, and he never loved anyone but your mother and you and somebody else who never was born. All of which made him an American uncle, I suppose.

Great Pyramid

You trudge home from work so tired that you enter the wrong house.

They lay you down like a child and kiss you

and fleece your pockets and steal your shoes.

But it matters only to the thieves. You are immortal

like a man crushed under a block in a great pyramid.

Demolition

That summer we tore out the whole bridge deck.

It was supposed to be work

but we laughed like horses, jitterbugged

with the jackhammers. We chiseled

the rotted concrete chunks under our shoes,

calling them by the various names

of cheaters we knew: Those home-busting

cowbirds who now kept their beer

in our old fridges, slept with our women, splashed

our cologne on their sticky faces in the morning.

This was some years before a doctor taught me

to manage fury like a checking account, spend a little

in one direction, more in another; long before

those arts-and-crafts lessons in the nuthouse

where I built a wooden hat rack for my ex-wife.

But Jesus, how we pound-pounded that bridge,

watched the concrete chunk-a-chunks

tumble through corroded rebar rods,

dropping thunk-a-*boom* to the gully below.

Insurance

The best apartment I could afford in that town
had crackling uncertain lights, and a coughing

furnace, the non-insurance that love buys
when it first comes barefoot into town.

The insurance man knocked on our door
and got us out of bed, wet with love.

There's no such thing as a good dog bite,
he said, standing in the door. I said, There's no dark
like the heart's fist that grabs the vodka.

We ate breakfast together, we three.
Then he climbed into our bed and curled up

like the donuts that diners sell to insurance men,
and my love and I went off to work.

Estate Sale

Why want? That is what we should ask ourselves; that is
the empty-house-and-barn of all our questions. You think

you can still find a horse in that shed. Think you can
still hatch eggs, that respect is about standing up when

all your accusers are dead and all principles have passed
through the pig. You think your house is merely old. That

civilization spreads in all directions from one sack
of testicles, a big bang from those old twin nuts that

founded the feast and ruled the farm from the mantle for
a hundred and sixty years. With all that history, why

want? Because want is made of want. It's a fact like rain
and sun, like nitrogen. It swims upstream, splits like a cell

and grows, and stinks after it dies in the weeds, out of which
new desires blossom. You want to keep this old boudoir? No,

you want only want. As do I. No one can take it from us—
the want, I mean. Let them have the damned furniture.

On Thumbs: After Montaigne

I had the hood up. I'd borrowed tools and spread
a Chilton manual on the bench (*simple*, right?),
war-paint of grease on my face. But do you think
I could tune that car, that son of a bitch? They finally
towed it away. I remember a Montaigne essay,
how galley slaves were kept from escape by cutting
off their thumbs so all they could do was row.
I should have learned such reliable work, I mean
the imperative rowing of things, the finger-smashing
hammer work, which all men should know:
skinning a cow, castrating a pig, sewing a new grid
of electric wires through an old plaster wall.

My father could do such headlong stuff: drive a truck
against the side of a leaning barn and knock it plumb,
catch the last crawdad in a dying pond, then say,
Now you try it. But God and my mother gave him
complicated sons who'd splice an orange to a mulberry bush,
splice an idea to a light to a kite, and reel in our hooks dripping
empty as question marks. So, from time to time he'd
strop his knife, and grinning, tell us to stick out our thumbs.

Mortifications

The Holy Re-runs

Moses still follows the night around and around

the earth, the reels of his epic movie under his arm

like stone tablets, no longer looking for the door

to the promised land, or promised souls.

His first-run days are as far behind him as Egypt.

And the man who played his part so well is dead.

Now he travels to old-run theaters, college film retrospectives

and Easter parties in Russia, Mumbai and Oklahoma,

looking for that old awestruck, chosen audience,

that generation who sat at their steering wheels

in drive-ins and smoked and watched the parting of the sea,

and took a hit from a bottle and said, *Oh, God.*

The Cold

Nature gave us furless hides so we'd huddle in the cold & reproduce. God also made us naked so that titillation would work in the warmer climes where He was from. Nature made us furless to develop our sense of touch. God made us nude for fear that we'd shit our pants. Go ahead & prove me wrong.

You'll Get Your Turn

My friends are dying. What do you say when this happens?
Give me a different day? One in which yearning itself keeps
you awake like a piranha hunting, rattled as a calf in a butcher's
wagon? So I say, "God, look, *behold*, my friends are dying."
And he says, "Don't worry, you'll get your turn, now go and live
your meanwhiles." "Ducks die every day," says the duck, "you're
yearning so inwardly that you havoc your guts." Where's that
waitress and that different day I asked her for? I want roasted
duck fresh from the hill, the one the sun is setting behind
so sullenly, where the buzzards dance in the air, the dogs
escort me growling, and the bulldozers come to cut their slice.

Famous singers die

so mysteriously sad, and you can name them all,
but lyrics survive to save your soul's genitals—.
Imagine one classic song that knew your name,
and it knew you were dying and it came to your bed,
and in sorrow you breathed out your soul into its arms like a new infant.

There's no heaven anymore, I'm told

and for years I've put off pondering where
my old ones took shelter after it ended, what

trillion-milepost inn, what Sakhalin of souls
received them—an awful scenario, and unfair,

especially remembering men who'd pray while
tying their shoes, who never ate a bean without

gratitude; remembering all their grim never-
nevers spoken to pleasure; remembering women

and men who walked to the woods by way
of Bethlehem, now somewhere hanging their

dispossessed coats. And that long-ago Stephen
(first-among-martyrs, for whom I was named,

who died under a riot of stones) must have
joined my old ones by now in my stead

in some shelter so far away they're safe from
anxious refuters like me who'd ruin them again.

All There Is

Time, like everything else, began in stone, till lightning struck
blowing a pollen of etcetera that started this eternity
in which we're sitting & talking.
But we're still fond of original stone because time has turned jittery now.
It picks fights with lovers, wrinkles them & walks away.
We make phone calls behind its back like it doesn't exist,
when of course it is really all there is.

Adam

You remember the woods east of town when I was its lone ascetic,

we kissed and held hands and the dark ate our clothes.

Can you believe in flute music and not in the flutist, asked the old sage.

Well, every woman who left me went to a man with more woods.

Two doubters on the river, I can't recall if it was Pison, Gihon or Hiddekel,

but we had it all to ourselves. And doubters love deeper, of that I am certain.

After Samson, blinded, pulls down the temple,

he wanders away through the other scriptures.
Still dazed, he hears the trumpet at Jericho and thinks,
finally, it's rescue divine. He hears the men who pisseth
against the wall and thinks he's reached the Fountain.
Any woman might be Delilah come to tell him she's
sorry, since everything is maybe until it's not.

Once he wanders into the Apocrypha and his story is offered
various other versions, one in which he keeps his sight but
no love, or he can keep his love but not his eyes, which
drives him away in a rage.

                                              Then someone, a tousled
magician (or who knows who—it's a land and time
when angels and dogs and assassins are co-indistinguishable,
but someone) gives him a light, like you'd touch a match
to another's cigarette; but this flicker rises like a moon
in his brainpan and shows him the way across the sands
of Deuteronomy, Second Samuel and Job. Now his
footprints mark a man in a hurry. He has a sister in Zorah
and a brother in Nimrud, if he can get to one of them
before the light goes out.

The Accidental Saint

He made it by performing a couple of miracles,
but he loathes to recall how unintentional they were:
a woman supposedly healed by his hands when he
only happened to fondle her at the moment
when her fever broke; a man he saved from the stake
merely by beating the Cardinal at poker.

And finally his martyrdom: losing his head on the block
(as it happened, on Good Friday) when he was
too old and fuzzy to understand his crime of muttering
in a bar about the King's divorce, his brain-load
of dulled erudition dropping to the bloody stones.

Now as saint he does what he's called on to do,
the holy patron who finds lost cats, mislaid reading glasses—
now that GPSs have taken lost drivers off his onus.
The last time he bellyached of boredom, they gave him
kids who lose their allowance in vending machines
(He even shakes the clumsy contraptions and curses for them).

Hell tried to hire him away, to confuse the tongues again
by spreading mayhem through the Internet. And true, hell

is a more interesting place. But, *weren't they insinuating that he's not a real saint, that Hell knows better?*

"Screw them," he told Wolsey and Luther. "Screw those devils."

Earth and Names

The earth and all our names are tired,

thus sayeth the fire to the window.

Our names have walked the roads, have

said themselves again and more,

turning the earth under their tread.

How often has the world said John

or Joshua, Mary or Eloise? They're all

back again for another whipping, back for

new bread: How far, Cain, can we

go with your name, mounting another

of history's horses? We're *tired*,

I'm telling you. I plead for a new name,

more and fresher alphabets to sing.

Late

My father drove us an hour and a half to Loew's Buffalo
where *Ben-Hur* was playing. But inside the lobby he cramped
to a halt—*No, hang it*, he would not money the palms
of philandering actors for glittering the Jesus story. He drove us
home again. It seemed late, though it wasn't. Our old dog
was howling at the wind and we went to bed without a word.
Piety is hard, you see. You wrestle with an angel in the dark
which turns out to be a tree, or your own leg. Eventually age
washes its hands of your sacrifices because it wants you whole.
But forty Easters later we watched the epic together on TV,
my father and me: the chariots and the healing, Pilate and the wind
and shadows on Golgotha. By now he'd forgotten his ticket-counter
paralysis just as he'd unremembered his road to this apartment
and all that he'd carried here— swept from his memory as if he'd
been healed of blindness and sores. It seemed late, and it was.

Mortification

I remember a crowd of barefoot people walking up

a brick street in Jamestown, the children sobbing,

wishing some sidewalk Lazarus would bless them with water.

Their mothers nudged them on while cars crept slowly around. Anyway,

sixty generations of songbirds later, those mothers must be dead.

The city paved over the bricks with asphalt.

The old stores closed, but new enterprises smile at you now,

and no one I know remembers that crowd I saw that day;

so, when I no longer remember, they'll have never existed,

their stubbed toes and cuffs rolled up, tender mothers with

a handkerchief, bloody prints on the bricks, no one remembering

that pain so sullen and lovely that I never forgot them.

Or Not

Our school burned down every June

its terrible smoke hanging over the corn,

and every September rebuilt,

    and so precisely

that only we pupils could tell

    its inexactitude:

an expletive not restored to a lavatory wall,

locker combinations confused,

some window gone wayward in its view.

Children were hunted down

and herded back from the woods.

Math and Latin reinvented

    each September,

history led back like a runaway cow.

And the man with the mop bucket,

duster of vomit, scrubber of glass,

    so much like the last

only we knew his stand-in status.

Now we hunt each other. Old kids

want to hear each other say

that we remember something

    of school

that no two people possibly can.

And anyway, *which* school? The one

that died of measles?

The one that apparently torched itself

in a wild act to purge us?

Or the one they rebuilt but forgot

the pencils, the faucets, forgot the walls.

We'd finally crossed the stage

      and out the door

with our diplomas when it caught ablaze

once more. But this time only we seniors

escaped. God warned us not to look back.

—For Winnie Rogers Smith

Brought in for Questioning

After my lover's murder the cops made me
look through a thousand pages of
moon mug-shots. Finally I saw the pic

of a red moon hiding half its face. That's the one,
I thought. But why tell them? *Let's talk
about that train*, the cops said. (I'd told them

already about the long freight crying through
the woods on the night in question.) What
train? I smirked now. They looked at each other.

What was it crying about? How should I
know? *Take him around the block*, said one
cop. *See if his memory improves*. But my

bad memories are like colds: they only improve
by going away. Cops are always pursuing
the moon but they never make an arrest,

so they pick on a train: make it panic and run
crying through the woods, while lovers lie
dead all over the world. I'm damned if I'll talk.

Homage to *The Night of the Iguana*

Just to escape banks and dodge the phones,

to turn traitor, or just to be an ass,

I'd drive an old bus down to Puerto Vallerta

like the Rev. Shannon in *Iguana*.

But I'd carry no one.

I'd run it up the side of a jungle hill

ramming and ramming

until mud is up to the door.

Then I'd sit at the wheel

and watch monkeys eyeing me until

steam stops blowing

out of the radiator, and the moon looks into

my side-view mirror. The eternal

jungle sounds. Bell of a poor church.

The ocean. My heart. Everyone wants to do this.

Or Not

I'm going to start my own Believe It or Not Museum. I have to

make a living. I'm short of bucks so I'll fill it

with things I can get for free. Like the bicycle I left in a field

where it was trampled by cows and ruined.

The ten-foot milk snake my mother killed with a hoe. The slippers

I wore home from the nut house. A thank you card

from a God representative. Carruth's clarinet—

well, no, I guess I gave that back. The hole in the floor of my first car.

Maurice Chevalier's autograph. The sleeping bag I lived in

when I was twenty-one. The rabbit I buried

in chisel-hard ground under snow, leaving its ears sticking out.

A booster shot that failed to make me grow.

The dog who coaxed me out of the house at midnight

to show me a bottomless hole in the barn floor.

The Hanukkah card I sent to Isaac Bashevis Singer,

which came back unopened. The Christmas card I sent

To Khrushchev—maybe I can get it back from the Kremlin archives.

The letter I wrote to Nixon but didn't mail.

A bodiless voice that chased me home from a funeral.

The bottle that came out of an alley and grabbed me, drove me all over the county from one party to another, then told me to come back tomorrow, same time, or it would kill me or someone I loved. Believe it or not. But you do, don't you?

Horses

To hell with horses. I always feel second to them, so graciously

muscled and arrogant. Whatever I do, a horse is always besting me.

My ex-wife rode them far and whinnying into the woods

and to the fields beyond, across unmapped roads.

To hell with riding lessons, I'm always thrown and left in the gravel.

Horses don't care that they're still living in some preindustrial age--

a coven of riders come pummeling over the hill, even while

Mars landings and Jupiter probes fill the internet news in tech-logos.

But our old root imagination that once made us, and our horses and dogs,

is always under hoof. I mean, my ex is still on a roan

with thunder overhead, bounding up from a glacial valley

on a primal air current that froths at its narrative of mane and loin,

forelock and flank. How in hell are we getting through this life

if we don't ride? And some just can't. I'm sorry.

What Did You Love about Your Town?

Oh, I guess the tactile sweetness of things, what else can I call it,
the myrtle, the violets, a treacle of dirt,
a sanguine worm in the fingers, & sure,
it was a good town we landed in after our family fled Buffalo.

A hobo in busted shoes walking the tracks in the blue dusk
waved to us boys. He carried a ragged suitcase,
begging our imagination about its contents,
though we knew it was nothing but dirty desultories.

All our family's Depression glass
was broken by then & now we ate off more solid Syracuse China.

Then came the amazing authority of snow
stripping humiliated trees— the possibilities of torment are endless,
which is natural, one comes to realize. I wanted to evolve
but we're hard-wired to pick ourselves out of a lineup:

I point at the one with the worm in his fingers,
or the *homme sérieux* with the suitcase,
but really, *really*, I expected others. I mean, I'd lived all that time.
That is why people pick the end of their lives first
& tell a story of what came before, its tactile sweetness, the violets.

A Lucky Man

All the women I loved were from drinking families,
maybe because I met them in bars late at night.
I remember how easy it was to abandon apartments
when all that I owned fit in the trunk of my car.
Once I had a rent dispute with my landlady & left
in the middle of the night, everything jammed into
two cardboard boxes & a suit case, & I felt badly later
because I hadn't cleaned the tub. But Zen Buddhists
taught me a chant that went, *All evil actions committed
by me since time immemorial*, & so on, finishing with,
I now repent having committed, & you repeat it like
Hail Marys & sometimes it helps. My Baptist family did
not drink. Ever. Plotinus says we have two parts to our
souls, the lower one that slogs with you through all
your quotidian mud, your sweet dreams & nightmares;
but the higher one, The Essential Soul, is the one
that we vaguely hope to ascend, wherein
is divinity, or peace anyway. Sometimes drinking
with a woman's partying family was like a collective
walk in the woods: being experienced drinkers,
they'd stop at some instinctive point, & I'd go on until
I'd realize I was alone in the dark. But a new drinker

from a dry tribe will finally understand, as I did,

that non-Baptists, I mean Methodists, Catholics, atheists

& the rest, do not necessarily get blasted every night, nor

tell dirty stories at dinner. It was the early church that

read Plotinus, certainly not the later Baptists or Pentecostals,

but people who still love him insist he was right that

Creation occurred when the *One* overflowed, or he

was in the way that I was right to overflow whenever

I fell in love, & he was a lucky man that he never found

out he was amiss, as I did so goddamned many times.

Safe

You used to be able to flag a ride in this country.

Impossible now—everyone is afraid

of strangers. Well, there was fear then too,

and it was mutual: drivers versus hitchhikers.

And we rode without seatbelts,

insurance or beliefs. People

would see me far ahead on a hill like a seedling,

watch me grow in the windshield

and not know they were going to stop until

they got right up to me. Maybe they wanted

company or thought I'd give them

some excitement. It was the age

of impulse, of lonesome knee jerks. An old woman

stopped, blew smoke in my face

and after I was already in her car she asked me

if I wanted a ride. I'm telling you.

Late one night a construction boss pulled over.

One of his crew had been hit

by the mob, he said as he drove, distraught

and needing to talk to someone.

We rode around for a long time.

He said, *I never wore a gun to a funeral before,*
but they've gotta be after me too.

Then he looked at me and patted the bulge

in his coat. *Don't worry,* he said, *you're safe.*

The Editor's Assistant

I was his chauffeur. Other times his
Earl of Kent, weather vane, game show host,
galley rower, his Prefect for

the Doctrine when rejections had to be sent.
I made his ticking martini bomb
from boar's head gin with a lamb's bleat

of vermouth. I erected his gate,
gatored his moat, confused the tongues
of people trying to tickle his ventricles.
Yet I was only his postman,

the one who rented his fuck movies,
rewrote the bungled blurbs by famous poets.
I was his pall bearer, and minutes later

his eulogist. Then I went home and growled
at everyone. Looking for something
to do, I put on his hat and went out again.

All Formulae Absent

The blue prayer the preacher offers at the funeral, mourners flipping coins in the parking lot, the rescuing tavern after interment, and your mother lying now underground in a strange light that is blue like the prayer, now you see her breast rise and fall, seeming about to wake, for the rest of your life.

Metastasis

Somewhere a condemned man has
for a fraction forgotten why he's

standing blindfolded, hearing: *Ready*!
An irking, beautiful word. What if

we could stop there, meditate on
Ready, could we endure it? Some-

where I stand dumb with a shovel
being told what to *Do*, a word so

guttural and sweet that it makes me
think vaguely of sex. What if you

could hold your favorite pain like
like a lover's sad head, instead of it

digging its heels into your ribs,
urging you toward a red, red dark.

Metastasis wears a cape and mask
and works all goddamned night

just to surprise you later, when for

a fraction you'll recall your final smoke,

the apology upon blindfolding: There

was nothing more anyone could *Do*.

Regarding the Old Faker

You've read of Onamacritos, ancient copier

& forger who altered & twisted Homer and Sophocles

to honor his clients: For a couple coins

he'd add your granddad's name to the siege of Ilium,

or your town's slovenly sailors to the Catalog

of Ships. For wine he'd slip your mother into a Pindar ode

as seamless as a marble nude, your new lover

into a Sapphic verse as easy as between

your sheets.
                      Inspired, you call

the International Star Registry with your

credit card & hang your lover's name on

a pin prick of celestial light. But don't admit

that her star was 19.95. Don't tell her it's been dead

since before Hammurabi, & Hubbell is just now

recording its final wink at eternity. Tell her she's immortal

now that she's mid-way between Marilyn's star

and Mata Hari's.

But you can't hide the heavens

from her forever, & when she finds out

your name will be pinned to one of her yesterdays,

growing fainter as her galaxy moves on.

Onamacritos got away

with it by keeping his edits modest. He did not

put his own lover in Olympian company, or tie her to

an alter for Agamemnon to butcher. "You're in

the Chorus," he told her. "Is that all?" she hollered. "I've

slept with you for seven years & all I get is

a mask?"

But their battles are

immortal. Students still translate her Doric curses,

his dactyls of defense & dissuasion. One

young man I know stuck with them all night,

his lexicon & verb charts sprawled on his desk

like togas flung until finally the old faker

lands her back in bed, but their names

are now Greg and Melissa, like the student & his lover,

participial- & subjunctive-ecstatic

as their stars dissolve to death in the morning sky.

Autumn Inventory

Home is that place where, when you have to go there,
They have to take you in.
                              —Robert Frost

The last spider web to snag my face,

Last flies and mosquitoes before the frost kills all.

The ground hog beat me

To the last tomatoes. What else should I count?

I'm at an age when my friends

Have filled their pots either with gold or shit, but know they're full

And are letting go, taking their seats

In the upper bleachers to watch

Others' games running later, the fireworks more distant.

But I keep turning my life over like a cold engine

Warming myself to an idea of morning

Like the frozen car radio revivifying in mid-tune.

A little cash in the bank, enough

Classes to teach, sure, I'll make it till spring. I've moved

Twenty times, give or take, following want ads like

Another reads Prince Valiant. So I don't know

Where I live, really. After half a century no one

Has to take me in anymore.

On the road I saw a Florida-bound truck overturned,
Its load of beehives scattered and busted, swarms
Migrating in desperation over the dry autumn fields.
Wouldn't it be funny to chase them?

A Long Day

I did so badly at my draft physical, they sent me to a psychiatrist
who had an office near the zoo. You could hear the elephants
trumpet as I walked in. Afterward I took a bus home,
and on the way two men got on carrying lunch buckets.
Loooong day, said one to the other. The doctor was
the Army's grand jury of one. My answers might mean my life.
I remember the elephant trumpets, but not the questions
he asked. I remember the man who said *Long day*,
but not my answers to the doctor's questions
that I can't recall. I remember a fight in a bar
where I got off the bus, two men beat each other senseless.
Then they sat down and laughed.

Poor

When I was poor I stole toilet paper & soap from
Gas station men's rooms. History, if it knew me at all
    would have forgiven me. But I knew
History for what it was, not a recital of causes
    as they claim, but woods
Old & rutty & fragrant, with the occasional epic fire.
    Food was much harder
To purloin than toiletry. Heat too—I left my door open to catch
A little from the hall. Yet, it was so lovely
To think only of *food* & *heat*, sit at my typewriter & bang out
    those two words, & hope that
Someone wouldn't come & step on them, take me
    away & feed & thaw me, & yet,
Dear God, how I *wanted*, & want pisses all over hope.
Well, I don't have to tell you that—want pisses on you too,
    & always will, & we like it, don't we?

Rolling Away

Lena's ex-husband came over one night and died on the couch.
Beautiful, right? Imagine how she felt. Never mind
how it rattled me. But he only died from the neck down,
his head was still telling army stories. We buried him standing up
in the garden with his head above ground, and we went inside
and shut the door. But his dome grew like a melon:
Gimme, gimme, nourish me. At night the moon laid its calming
hands on his swelling brow. But in the day? I spent hours
weeding around his jowls, giving him shaves, scrubbing
his ears, letting him air his laments about Lena.
Soon I had to climb a ladder to give him a haircut.
Lena and I were making love one night when a windstorm
struck, and we heard him scream: His head broke off
from the ground like a puff ball, rolling over the fields.
I pulled on my pants and chased him. But Lena didn't even get up.
What was I supposed to do when I caught him?

Feral

You gave your first heart to a field mouse.
People say their first love came as a bolt of light.
But yours was that feral thing you put in your shoe,
and saved it from a dog. What other love
gave you such satisfaction? It was your second heart
and your third and fourth you gave when you
tried to conjure lightning like an apprentice to a holy man.
One woman you loved like that field mouse:
you put her in your car and saved her from a brute
in a bar where she'd been drinking. She read
Sappho when she wasn't on a barstool, but she
could no more love you than the field mouse could,
or she loved you the way she loved Channel 7
when she was a kid—the Saturday morning cartoons—
and she couldn't make love to you any more
than she could to the television. This is the history
that you bring to your next attempt at love. The
field is wet, there is a moon, and the heart is feral.

Sometimes I forget the universe and wander the ocean floor

amid coral and mud, the masts of sad ships, eerie luminous fish and squid,

skeletons with ankle chains or wrapped in flags, cannon balls,

nuclear offal in crusted barrels, a sextant or two, a sunken circus boat

with lion skulls and whips, and in the most frigid depths a window

to a first class cabin where a man and woman float naked, still coupled

as they were when a torpedo struck, her face still asking: *What the hell*

was that? And he: *It's nothing, dear, we probably ran over a fishing boat.*

Also, fallen booster rockets, crocks of ancient wine. The *Thresher*'s rudder.

And east of Gibraltar, a few leagues north of Saint-Exupéry's plane

dark and standing on its nose, is a ship laden with the rescued drama

section of the Alexandria library, the face carved on the bow still asking:

Is everything lost? The usual question. But my lungs are always

exhausted by the time I reach this boat, because nowadays even

in dreams I'm short winded. But I can give you a map writ in water.

A Flying Fish

Ammons said the time to write a poem is when you have nothing
to say. When I have nothing to say (even when the Kepler space
ship sends back shots of Jupiter like an excited tourist
with an expensive camera, when I sat on Rexroth's grave
and watched the waves slapping the Santa Barbara shore,
when St. John said, *En arche hn o logos*, when I was in a plane
with a junior pilot who couldn't land the damned thing,
when Armstrong stepped down the ladder, when my car
hit a long patch of ice, when I heard the guns of Attica blast
a mile away, when I fell from a bridge on a pile of rubble
and got up and walked, when I realized I had lost everything
until I stared at my hands, when I heard Lead Belly sing
In the pines in the pines where the sun never shines),
I admit I can't add much. Is a poem like a flying fish
in love with the moon? Am I too late in the world to say?

About the Author

STEVEN HUFF is the author of two books of poetry, most recently *More Daring Escapes* (Red Hen, 2008), and two collections of stories, *Blissful and Other Stories* (Cosmographia, 2017), and *A Pig in Paris* (Big Pencil, 2008). He is editor of *Knowing Knott: Essays on an American Poet* (Tiger Bark, 2017). Recent essays have appeared in *The Gettysburg Review* and the *Solstice Literary Magazine*. He is a Pushcart Prize winner in fiction and an O. Henry finalist. He is working on a travelogue, *In Our Home Ground: Journeys to the Grave Sites of Authors in Upstate New York*. The former Publisher at BOA Editions, Ltd., he is now Founding Publisher and Editor at Tiger Bark Press. He teaches creative writing at the Solstice Low-Residency MFA Program at Pine Manor College in Boston. He lives in Rochester NY.

Acknowledgements

I gratefully acknowledge the editors and publishers of the publications where some of the poems herein, or earlier versions thereof, were first published:

2River View: "Famous Singers Die," and "In the Hall of Rashes";

The Chautauqua Review: "Safe," also selected by Ted Kooser for the syndicated *American Life in Poetry*

The Comstock Review: "Late," and "A Long Day";

Malpais Review: "Brought in for Questioning";

Many Mountains Moving: "Estate Sale";

Redactions: "There's no heaven any more, I'm told";

Stone Canoe: "Insurance," and "A Fire in the Hill";

Stray Dogs (anthology edited by William Hastings): "An American Uncle," and "Demolition."

San Pedro River Review: "Horses," as "To Hell with Horses," and "What Did You Love about Your Town?"

Two Rivers Review: "The Editor's Assistant," and "Homage to Night of the Iguana."

www.ingramcontent.com/pod-product-compliance
Lightning Source LLC
Chambersburg PA
CBHW020958090426
42736CB00010B/1374